Surviving an Emergency

Bill Snyder

FOOD AND WATER STORAGE AND OTHER PREPARATION TIPS
FOR THE URBAN DWELLER

LUMINARE PRESS

WWW.LUMINAREPRESS.COM

Surviving an Emergency

Copyright © 2019 by Bill Snyder

Printed in the United States of America

Cover Design by Claire Flint Last

Luminare Press
442 Charnelton St.
Eugene, OR 97401
www.luminarepress.com

ISBN: 978-1-64388-083-9

TABLE OF CONTENTS

Introduction

I magine, for a moment, that, without warning, you cannot go to a grocery or hardware store, or a gas station. They're closed- all of them, with virtually no notice. Taking care of yourself and your family through a brief, local power outage is hardly a life threatening situation. After all, the power will be back on in a few minutes, or a few hours, or, on a rare occasion, a day or two. A seldom occurring exception are the instances where massive storms cause power outages for days or weeks, events that effect a relatively small population of the American public, and then, only infrequently.

There are other possible scenarios which could be much more lengthy than a local power outage and the chances of one or more of those occurring become more likely with each passing day. Is this the month, or the year, when a massive swath of the American power grid is sabotaged? Or will this be the year when a hostile nation manages to destroy or damage our satellite system? Think about that one- everything would come to a halt. Freight, whether truck or rail, would stop, credit cards, computer access, among others, would be everyday functions that no longer existed.

The pages that follow will prepare you for catastrophic events that might last for weeks or months. Regardless of the duration, being caught in an unplanned disaster with no preparation is hardly imaginable. Following the detailed planning in this book will keep you and your family alive, allowing time to make decisions about sheltering in place or changing locations.

It is also worth noting that the simple *threat* of a catastrophic event would be enough impetus for mobs of people to empty store shelves in a matter of hours. If, for example, the imminent (or actual) possibility of a nuclear strike against another country were to happen, the simple idea that that event had the likelihood of triggering a wider conflict would be enough to send urban populations into an immediate panic. Many people scoff at the idea that a widespread, national emergency is possible. The reality is that an outbreak of a lethal disease like Ebola could cause widespread panic, even though it is halfway across the country. Nor should we discount the value of a well- stocked pantry in the event of sudden job loss or an uninsured injury or illness.

FOOD

FOOD STORAGE

An effective food storage program involves some planning beyond occasionally throwing a few extra cans of food in a kitchen cupboard. Having a dedicated space is essential, whether it's an already existing pantry, a small closet, or a portion of a larger closet or some open shelving in a spare room. Another focus is stock-piling foods that you and your family will eat, with careful attention to any diet restrictions you or a family member might have.

An important consideration when you begin, is paying attention to the shelf life of any particular item. If you want long term storage of high protein, canned food, tuna fish and sardines are at the top of the list. Both have storage lives that are typically around two years; other essential canned foods are fruit and vegetables, with a focus on those that are family favorites. Foods to avoid are baked goods such as chips and crackers, the exception being a few packages that might be used quickly in the instance of an emergency that lasts only a few days. For families of three or more consider buying often used items by the case.

> **TIP:** On numerous occasions the author has been shown well-stocked pantries that are incomplete in a very important respect. Do you have cats, dogs, or other pets that are part of your family? Stock adequate wet and dry food that will last them for an extended period of time.

>

This pantry is five shelves, with a width of approximately three feet. Completely stocked, it can support a family of four for a month or longer.

Any food storage program should be implemented with the idea that an emergency could last for an extended period of time; with that in mind, pay attention to any canned food item that has a 'Best By' date that is a year or longer. There is also a place in any storage program for dry foods that can be used and easily replaced, such as high quality dry items like oatmeal, wheat and grain cereals, including soup mixes. Leaving dry foods in their sealed packages and putting them in gallon zip lock bags or plastic containers will extend their shelf life, minimizing any oxidation of contents when tiny, virtually invisible punctures are present.

Bill Snyder

Become a shelf life expert- with the thousands of items available in any large grocery store, you have access to your own research laboratory, going from aisle to aisle and spending a few extra minutes with every visit to look at 'use by' and 'best by' dates on the packaging. (End dates on packaging are not cut in stone- as long as containers/packaging is not damaged, products can be used weeks/months beyond the marked dates.) As mentioned above, be aware of any food restrictions for anyone in your family that involve carbohydrate and sodium levels.

Some labels take a bit of deciphering, such as the one at top of photo. (Best By is April 2020) Many others are easy to read, as illustrated by can at bottom of photo.

Various print and online publications mention foods like soybeans, dry pasta, wheat and dried corn, along with other food items, as having indefinite shelf lives; those recommendations presuppose certain conditions. If you are able to store those foods in a dark area, using double containers (plastic containers with tight, snap fit or threaded lids, or wide mouthed glass containers with screw lids) and live in a cool climate, the usable life of many dry foods is greatly increased. There will also be left over amounts of dry foods like pasta and noodles that you may need to store for only hours or a day or two – keep a supply of quart and gallon zip locks bags on hand for those items.

A PARTIAL LIST OF HIGH PROTEIN FOODS

(This list is a starting place to begin a storage program of high protein items that includes some dry foods that have a shorter shelf like than most of their canned counterparts.) Note: The author recently used a package of elbow macaroni that was two years past its Best-By date. After carefully inspecting the contents for insect damage and any perforation of the packaging, the product was cooked and used.

1. Canned Tuna (packed in water, not oil)
2. Canned Sardines (also packed in water)
3. Canned Chicken (brand shop for low sodium)
4. Canned Beans (especially black beans)
5. Dry Oats (many varieties available)
6. Lentils and chickpeas (add to simple soups and stews)

ADDITIONAL CANNED AND DRY PRODUCTS

1. Canned vegetables such as peas, corn, green beans. Include nutritionally complex items such as beets

2. Refried beans, condensed milk (canned) tomato and pasta sauces (canned or glass)

3. Peanut butter, almond butter

4. Dry packaged items like noodles, navy and pinto beans, flour and rice, soup mixes

5. Good quality granola and trail mix

Beans are available in many varieties, are high in protein and can easily be added to simple soups and stews. Shelf life of most canned beans is around two years.

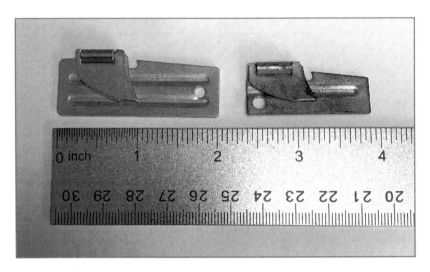

The p-51 on left, and its smaller cousin, the p-38, have been around for decades. These small can openers are always useful, whether in a pantry or in your pocket. Hard to imagine a more perfect barter item in a prolonged emergency.

A NOTE ABOUT POTATOES

Feeding four or more people can quickly deplete food supplies. Potatoes are one way to have an inexpensive and supplemental food on hand. A medium potato has around 35 grams of carbohydrates and a scant 160 calories. That same medium potato also has over four grams of protein and a high content of vitamin c and potassium. Using nothing more than a propane burner or barbeque, potatoes can be cooked in a variety of ways, as well as being supplements in soups and stews. The secret for storing potatoes is cool, dark and dry. Potatoes need ventilation and should never be stored in closed containers. Purchase 10 to 20 pounds of potatoes (or more) and sort them by hand, making sure they are all dry and discard any that are bruised or damaged. A basement or cellar make ideal storage, (potatoes keep best at 40 – 45 degrees) and if that is not an option, store them in the coolest place in your house such as a dry, dark closet. Properly stored, potatoes will last months, especially if you do periodic checks and remove any that have soft spots or are otherwise damaged. Using stored potatoes and replacing them as you go will ensure a continual supply of a highly nutritious addition to your emergency food stores.

A cut-away view of potatoes stored in layers, using cardboard (or newspaper). In cool temperatures and well ventilated, these potatoes will keep for an extended period of time. See text for details.

COOKING METHODS

People who live in densely populated areas rarely own, or have access to portable generators. Gas engines produce exhaust, are not quiet, and require the continual replenishing of gasoline. In rural areas, where gas can be easily stored and neighbors are not present to be disturbed by the noise, generators offer many possibilities; for our purposes, small propane burners offer a viable solution. Propane, properly handled, with undamaged tanks and accessories, is as safe as any other heat source. Although propane burners should never be used indoors, porches, patios and garages, if well vented, are good choices for propane use. Food and water can be quickly heated, allowing anyone to cook simple meals. If you decide to buy a full-size propane stove, regardless of size and cost, just be aware that portability is no longer an option.

This propane burner, shown with five-gallon tank is housed in a metal frame about 14" high and is one of the many different types of propane burners available.

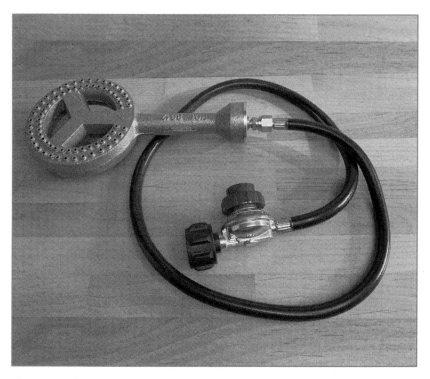

This small propane burner, equipped with a five-foot hose, is lightweight and portable.

TIP: *If you have never used propane, purchase a single or double burner, connecting hose and tank at a local sporting goods, or hardware store, rather than online. Find a store employee and have them show you, in minute detail, how the hose connections are made, how to light the burner and regulate the simple propane tank valve. If any part of the process is not clear, ask questions. Most store employees are more than happy to share their familiarity with these kinds of products.*

Another possibility is a propane or briquette barbeque. Either of these can be used to generate adequate heat to boil water and cook simple foods. Briquettes burn quickly- buy several large bags, ensuring a cooking method until the supply is gone. Propane is also easily stored and has a much longer storage life than other fuels such as gasoline. Propane also has the advantage of being available in different size containers, from small, 1 lb. bottles, up to 5 gallons, (and larger) though full, 5 gallon containers are quite heavy. Other options include one and two gallon containers which are readily available. Not using propane indoors also includes not storing propane indoors. Small, exterior storage areas that can be locked, inside a garage or other covered areas, are good choices. Many different foods using minimal ingredients can be prepared with a single propane burner; sample recipe possibilities are provided in the following pages.

Perhaps you already have a two burner propane camp stove with a folding lid. They are a common item in many homes and have been in periodic use over many years. If you have one of these units which has been stored away in basement or attic, now is the time to make sure that it is in good, usable condition. And, for everyone who has, or intends to acquire a propane unit, having a second one as backup is never a bad idea.

> **TIP:** *Many, if not most, people who have two burner camp stoves use them with the small, 1 lb. bottles for which they were intended. If you have never used any propane canister other than the small 'camping' size bottles, and want to use your camp stove for possible emergencies, consider the use of larger containers, such as five gallons, you will need an adapter hose, as the connector for the 1 lb. bottle is a slightly different fitting. Any store that sells propane equipment will normally have them in stock.*

FOOD PREPARATION

What follows are not actually recipes, but merely suggestions, and will give many readers endless ideas of how to prepare simple foods with a minimum of ingredients, while at the same time using as little fuel as possible.

1. One package of soup mix, prepared with quantity of liquid provided with the directions. If larger quantity is desired, add extra water (or canned broth) along with a can or two of corn, peas, or green beans.

2. Cook two cups of white rice in water, serve in bowls with canned, condensed milk and brown sugar. (Brown sugar stores well, even after package is opened, provided its kept is a glass jar with tight lid, or plastic container with snap or threaded lid.)

3. Cook egg noodles per package directions, reduce heat and add canned (or jar) white or red sauce, then stir in canned chicken, beef, or tuna. (Read labels on canned meats before purchase; canned meats, especially beef, can have very high sodium content.)

TIP: *If you must leave cooked foods on warm after cooking is completed, do so for the shortest possible time. If you're using a five gallon propane canister an average of one to two hours a day, it will last only a week or less, varying somewhat with each individual cooking style. Another method of conserving propane or other fuel is to immediately put excess soups or stews in wide-mouth thermos type containers.*

WATER STORAGE

Water is, along with a basic food supply, the most important item in your emergency storage program. Though
water is easy to store, the containers require a great deal
of space. The two methods of storing water are purchas-
ing sealed containers or filling empty containers from your tap.
Pre-packaged, four or six count one gallon blister packs are
readily available in many retail outlets and have the advantage of
being stacked several cases high. If you choose to fill your own
containers, use a variety of sizes. One and two gallon containers
are easy to use- five gallon containers are heavier than many
people want to handle. (Water weighs in at a little over eight
pounds per gallon.) If you're filling your own containers, make
sure they are food- grade quality. A small amount of liquid dish
soap should be used, with clean water, to wash the containers,
followed by sanitization with one teaspoon of liquid household
bleach, per quart of water. Once your sanitizing solution is
drained from the container, fill with fresh, clean water and seal
tightly. Also, do not neglect juice products (whether in plastic
or glass) which have an average shelf life of a year or so, if kept
out of excessive light and as cool as possible.

There is no simple answer to the question of how much water
is enough – it is much like the question of how much food to store.
The answer to both questions is obviously dependent on how long
emergency conditions last. Having enough food and water for a
week is certainly less problematic than acquiring supplies that must

last for a month or more, though it is not unusual to find households of three or four people where the choice is to reach a goal of food and water that will last for two months or longer.

Different households will have different water requirements. A starting place is using a multiplier of one gallon of water per day, per person. That only includes enough water for drinking and cooking. In a real, prolonged emergency, using water to constantly flush toilets or wash dishes is simply not a possibility. It is also important to rotate water supplies – whether you're using pre-packaged water or filling your own containers, replenish the supply every four months, if possible, definitely no longer than six months.

An ideal way to store pre-packaged water is in blister packs of four or six (shown) gallons.

Bill Snyder

*A variety of sizes in water bottles is helpful, Shown
here are half-gallon, one gallon and two gallon.*

TIP: *Along with your food and water supply, add packaged paper plates, plastic bowls and plastic silverware
– this will eliminate the nuisance of stacks of unwashed
dishes. Used paper plates can easily be disposed of
in large, sealable trash bags which should also be on
your list. A single package of 50 or 100 count bags
should be more than adequate.*

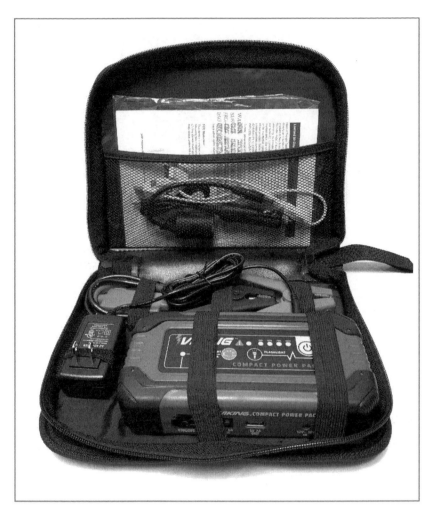

This power pack is an essential item in any emergency situation. Multi-function units like the one shown can hold a charge for up to six months.

ALTERNATIVE POWER SOURCES

oss of electricity for an indefinite period of time is one of the most difficult problems you will encounter in the event of a prolonged emergency. Lights don't work, you have no hot water and all the large and small appliances you have come to rely on no longer function. As previously mentioned, generators that rely on gasoline as a fuel source are impractical in many urban environments. Even if you do invest in a small generator, storing enough gasoline can be problematic. A generator is worth considering if you live in a single family dwelling with covered, well ventilated space. A supply of five gallon cans of gasoline, (or even a fifty gallon drum with hand pump) would provide, depending on the size of the generator, electricity until the fuel supply was exhausted. On the other hand, urban settings such as apartment houses would find this to be a virtually impossible solution.

Living for an extended period of time without normal household electricity is difficult but not impossible. There are some light weight, highly functional devices that alleviate some of the problem, one of them being a portable power pack. There are a variety of these units available online and at many specialty retail outlets. These little units weigh in at a pound or two and have the ability to jump start a vehicle and charge cell phones and other devices that use USB cords. Before you buy a power pack, read user reviews and understand the functions and capabilities of the unit you're considering. Some, for example, do not have the auto battery jump start function, a feature that could definitely be a life-saver under certain conditions. One of the important features of these units is their ability to hold a charge for up to six months. Also, if at all possible, avoid buying the lowest priced models. The author uses a power pack that was in the seventy five dollar price range and it has so far functioned with no issues.

TIP: *If you use any devices that function with non-standard USB cords, purchase an adapter that will allow connection to your power pack.*

There are also a number of small devices that can play an essential role in getting you through a crisis. Some of these are everyday items that are often taken for granted. Can you find a good quality flashlight with a moment's notice? And, should that light fail, do you have a backup? Buy the best LED flashlights you can afford, lights that use readily available batteries, and while you're at it, pick up several packages of high quality batteries. Additionally, buy a minimum of one 'pop-up' light. The LED versions of these lights often have high, medium and low settings, which allows some control over battery life. The 'pop-up' name stems from the mechanism which allows the light to be turned on and off by merely grasping the top and bottom of the light to pull it open (on) or collapse the light to turn it off. If this style of light is not to your liking, there are numerous other sizes and styles, easily found on the internet. Again, choose carefully, and always read the reviews. It's also worthwhile to purchase at least one flashlight that has a Velcro covered top and in a lightweight case that has a belt-loop.

TIP: *Search for "camping lanterns" on the internet, which will pull up many examples of pop-up style lights. Pop-up camping lanterns have a huge advantage over directional lanterns which can only throw light from one side of the unit, much like a flashlight. With their 360 degree light throw, a pop-up style lantern can light up an entire room without the need to be turned in one direction or another.*

Pop-up lights such as this one are small, lightweight and amazingly bright. Many use non-standard, rechargeable batteries. Check battery type before purchase. Small rechargers are very handy, as many will recharge several different size of batteries.

High quality flashlights are especially useful, whether pocket size, or with lanyard or belt pouch.

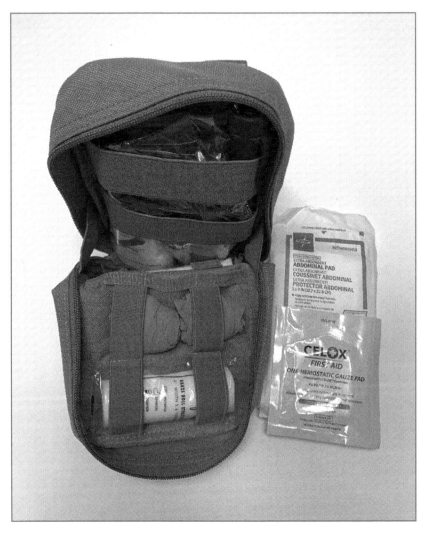

Add your own first aid essentials to this trauma kit.
It measures approx. 8"X10" with zippered enclosure.

ESSENTIAL FIRST-AID
SUPPLIES

I f the extent of your first-aid supplies consist of a couple of band-aids in a bathroom drawer, now is the time to make some changes. First aid kits are available in many retail outlets, and many are completely inadequate for dealing with serious, life threatening situations. Shop in-person or online (which usually offers better, more cost effective choices.) and find a trauma kit that has compression bandages, a tourniquet and blood-clotting gauze. You can add the size of small band-aids, a tube of antibiotic ointment and any other small first-aid items you may routinely use. Add to this kit the over the counter medications you like and keep all of these items in the trauma kit, preferably one which has a zipper closure.

> **TIP:** *If mention of compression bandages, blood-clotting gauze, etc., seems daunting, (especially if you have never had a first-aid course) use of none of these items require you to have a medical degree. Take advantage of local first-courses, widely available in most parts of the country, often free of charge. In lieu of that (or in addition) look at the many online videos which offer step-by-step use of simple medical items that would allow you to save your, or someone else's life.*

IF YOU HAVE TO CHANGE LOCATIONS

Make no mistake, the atmosphere in a dense, urban environment that is deprived of electricity, food shipments, and other essentials, could become very dangerous in a short period of time. If you are not trained and properly equipped to defend your space, be prepared to react quickly. (Many people in an urban environment which was in the grips of chaos would quickly opt to change locations where relatives or friends offered a more defensible position, whether a few blocks or miles away.)

Basically, there are only two scenarios in which location change happens. First, is the, 'Looks like we're ok for a day or two.' The second scenario is, 'We have to go *now!*'

If you find yourself in the second scenario, preparation is simple and essential. A sturdy backpack or canvas bag with a shoulder strap is the starting place. Choose something that has a 20 to 24 inch depth and a cross section in the range of 10 or 12 inches. (Smaller bags won't hold everything you need and larger bags quickly become unwieldly and too heavy to manage and carry easily.)

Stock your bag or backpack with a change of clothes and any extra items you commonly use that you don't have to access on a daily basis. Add to this, a few cans of high protein foods such as canned tuna, chicken and sardines; And now comes the important part – work from a short list which is always kept in the same place. That list covers the things that you use daily or aren't comfortable leaving in a bag that is exposed to anyone who happens to be in your house. Your list might look something like this;

1. Prescription medication
2. Passport
3. Envelope with spare cash
4. Flashlight

A few cans of high protein foods such as tuna, chicken or sardines should be kept in your quick exit bag.

If you're unsure about your ability (and safety) to shelter in place for a long period of time, and have access to another location, there's a few things to keep in mind. First, consider storing some of your food supplies in sturdy, easy to carry boxes. The necessity of changing locations with very little notice will allow food supplies to be taken with you if they are already in boxes that can be quickly loaded into a vehicle. Another consideration is gasoline- if you're one of those people who chronically operates a vehicle with a nearly empty tank, realize that in a widespread emergency gas supplies would almost instantly vanish. Also, keep an empty two gallon gas can in your vehicle. You can't barter, buy, or sell an emergency ration of gas if you don't have a container. A two gallon supply would allow an average forty or fifty mile range of movement. Five gallon gas cans take a lot of space, so have them as backup only if you anticipate the need to travel a long distance.

Do you have trusted friends or family nearby? In the event of a real, long-term emergency think about whether those people should be in your location, or you in theirs. Have those discussions now – do not wait until communication and movement are problematic or impossible.

Finally, do not procrastinate. Even if on a small scale initially, begin a storage and planning program as outlined in these pages. Most people who start these programs feel a sense of empowerment and accomplishment – after all, you're doing something that keeps you and your family prepared for virtually any eventuality that may appear with little or no warning.

NOTES

NOTES

NOTES

NOTES

NOTES

NOTES

Made in the USA
Columbia, SC
24 March 2019